The Easiest Learning There Is!!

"This book performs an extraordinary public service ..."

Richard Blumenthal
Connecticut Attorney General

"I've tracked Jimmy's incredible run of successful real estate investments for twenty years."

Jeff Dunne, Vice Chairman, CB Richard Ellis

"Don't let the stick figures fool you ... Jim Randel will have you laughing and thinking at the same time. A very enjoyable read!"

Ken Blanchard, author
The One Minute Manager®

"I love this book. It can literally save you a fortune!"

Gerri Detweiler, National Credit Card Expert

The Easiest Learning There Is!!

"What a funny and insightful book! Terrific observations!!!"

Dave Boone, Hollywood Comedy writer, Dancing With The Stars

"A terrific road map to online dating that is also a fun read!"

Jan Yager, Ph.D., author of the international bestseller, *125 Ways to Meet the Love of Your Life*

www.theskinnyon.com

The Skinny on Direct Sales

the skinny on™

direct sales
your first
100 days

Jim Randel

ISBN: 978-0-9824390-9-8
Library of Congress: 2009909972

Illustration: Malinda Nass

For information address RAND Publishing, 265 Post Road West,
Westport, CT, 06880 or call (203) 226-8727.

The Skinny On™ books are available for special promotions and premiums.
For details contact: Donna Hardy, call (203) 222-6295 or visit our website:
www.theskinnyon.com

Printed in the United States of America

the skinny on™

Welcome to a new series of publications entitled **The Skinny On**™, a progression of drawings, dialogue and text intended to convey information in a concise and entertaining fashion.

In our time-starved and information-overloaded culture, most of us have far too little time to read and absorb important writings and research on topics of interest to us. So, our understanding tends to float on the surface – without the insights of leaders and teachers who have spent years studying these topics.

Our series is intended to address this situation. Our team of readers and researchers has done a ton of homework preparing our books for you. We have read everything we could find on the topic at hand and have spoke with the experts. Then we mixed in our own experiences and distilled what we have learned into this "skinny" book for your benefit.

Our goal is to do the reading for you, cull out what is important, distill the key points and present them in a book that is both instructive and entertaining.

Although minimalist in design, we do take our message very seriously. Please do not confuse format with content. The time you invest reading this book will be paid back to you many, many times over.

INTRODUCTION

By reason of the fact that this book is in your hands, I am assuming that you have either decided, or are seriously considering, launching your own direct sales business. Congratulations, you are entering the world of entrepreneuring where your results are directly tied to your individual efforts.

As you will note, the subtitle of this book is "Your First 100 Days." We have called out the first 100 days because it is the most critical period of your new endeavor. Many people who begin direct sales either quit or go dormant (and never really wake up) in their first 100 days.

This book will explain why, and will help you not only make it through this period but also set the foundation for real success in the years to come. Let me state right up front that although we at **Skinny On** books have been educated about direct sales by some of the most knowledgeable people in the industry, we are not "shilling" for the direct sales business. We are not funded by any direct sales company. Our goal is to give you the facts. To help you be the best you can be.

So, just give us an hour or so of your time to follow the story of our hero and heroine, Billy and Beth. Billy is the breadwinner in the family and although Beth works part time, he makes all the financial decisions for the family. That is about to change.

In the pages following, we use the pronouns "she" and "her" more often than we use "he" and "him." That is because most direct salespeople are women (85%) although we are aware that increasing numbers of men are entering the business.

"(T)here are vast numbers of financial opportunities available to those who want one, and who are open-minded to doing something a little different. There are numerous part-time, home-based businesses ... fun, easy, and require no more than a few hours a week. In addition, many of these businesses require very little initial cash to get into and no prior experience.

"So what's the catch? ... As is so often the case, fear and worry are the greatest dream snatchers."

Don't Worry, Make Money, Richard Carlson

Hi, I'm Jim Randel and I am your moderator. At times I will jump in and out of the story (right up to the edge of being obnoxious ... **I hope**).

MEET BILLY AND BETH. THEY HAVE BEEN MARRIED TWELVE YEARS. THEY HAVE TWO CHILDREN, A 10-YEAR OLD SON AND AN EIGHT-YEAR OLD DAUGHTER. BILLY IS AN ACCOUNTANT AND THE BREADWINNER IN THE FAMILY. BETH WORKS PART-TIME IN A JEWELRY STORE. SHE DOESN'T MAKE MUCH MONEY.

2

"Sorry, Beth, I have to cut back your hours. Sales have been a bit off of late."

Of course they are... our product isn't great and you don't seem to be paying attention to the store.

3

BETH IS AT AN IMPORTANT CROSSROADS IN HER LIFE. SHE IS WORKING FOR SOMEONE WHO, FRANKLY, SHE DOES NOT RESPECT. SHE FEELS SHE CAN DO BETTER BUT DOES NOT HAVE THE CAPITAL NOR THE EXPERTISE TO OPEN HER OWN STORE

BETH'S FRIEND JAYNI HAS BEEN TALKING TO HER ABOUT DIRECT SALES. BETH IS SERIOUSLY THINKING ABOUT IT AS SHE LIKES THE IDEA OF CONTROLLING HER OWN DESTINY. BETH IS THINKING OF BECOMING AN ENTREPRENEUR!

ENTREPRENEUR
(from the old French, entreprendre, meaning "one who undertakes")

"A person who assumes the organization, management and risks of a business enterprise."

I will disclose a bias that I do have. I have been an entrepreneur all my life and I love entrepreneurs. Entrepreneurs are responsible for their own destiny. If things don't work out for them they have no one to blame but the person in the mirror. To some people that is frightening, to others it is exhilarating.

Being an entrepreneur is not about higher education. Here is what it is about:
1. Determination
2. Work ethic
3. Passion
4. Desire to be your own boss
5. Desire to be rewarded commensurate with your individual effort
6. Tenacity and persistence

Beth is considering starting her own business:

BETH, INC.

No longer will she be able to blame her income on her boss at the jewelry store. At the same time, she will no longer receive a salary. Her income will be tied directly to her effort.

There are no guarantees for the entrepreneur. However, for most, the graph that tracks their income looks like this:

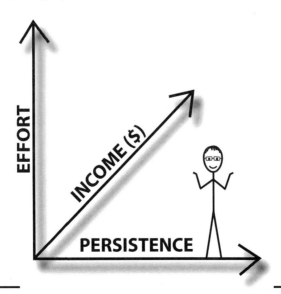

Since you are holding this book in your hand you are thinking about opening your own business too:

YOU, INC.

One of the goals of this book is to help you make YOU, INC. as successful as possible.

WARNING

1. Entrepreneuring is NOT for everyone. Being an entrepreneur means being PROACTIVE, not REACTIVE. In other words, an entrepreneur has to get up every day with the intention of making things happen. That is a lot different than working for someone else who tells you exactly what to do ... in the latter example, you REACT to instructions and demands from others.

2. There are many ways to be an entrepreneur. Some folks are full time – working every free hour they have. Others fit entrepreneurial activities within their other obligations and commitments. There is no one right way. The success or failure of YOU, INC. depends on the energy and commitment you invest in your business.

LET'S CHECK BACK IN WITH BILLY AND BETH

"Billy, I've been thinking about getting into direct sales."

14

15

16

17

For a great book explaining the different communication styles of men and women, see **Men are from Mars, Women are from Venus** by John Gray (Penguin, 2000).

We here at **The Skinny On** book series are aware that today about 15% of all new direct sales consultants are men. It's just that women actually tend to listen when men speak.

On the other hand, Beth was not exactly forthcoming with Billy. She has already committed to a direct sales company and has purchased a starter kit. Soon she will be selling.

As with any new venture, there is an initial period which will have a lot to do with whether the venture lives or dies. We have selected the first 100 days of a person's entry into direct sales as the critical period. What happens during that period will have a tremendous impact on not only whether YOU, INC. succeeds or fails, but also what level of success YOU, INC. achieves over the long term.

As part of our research for this book, we have spoken with many direct sales consultants who not only survived their first 100 days, but also used that period to create a foundation for a significant, long-term successful career.

We have identified what works and what doesn't. We have talked with them about techniques and mind sets. We have discussed the pressures and uncertainties a new consultant faces. We have tried to isolate those steps a new consultant should take in order to maximize his or her prospect for success.

"Billy, what is the name of the man who takes care of our lawn?"

"His name is Billy."

"Direct sales just means I market and sell products directly to people I know and meet. I don't have to work in a store. I don't have to work for someone else. I can work my own hours and I don't get paid by the hour."

"Yes, and you don't get a paycheck every week. You don't have a storefront for people to see your products. Your work day doesn't stop when the store closes. What about the kids? What about me?"

"Billy, I have thought a lot about this. I do know the negatives. But the kids are at the point where they don't need as much of my attention these days, and I would like to start making some real money. It's a little tough on minimum wage."

"I am doing OK, Beth. We don't need extra money."

The story of each sales consultant is unique; perhaps your reasons for entering direct sales are similar to Beth's. While Billy indicates that their family does not need "extra money," Beth would love to provide the funds for a family vacation – a trip that Billy doesn't think they can afford this year.

Even if one's family doesn't need extra money, many direct sales consultants enter the business to have their own income, independent of their spouse.

32

According to the information we have received, the three most often cited reasons for people entering the direct sales field are:

1. To make **one's own** money – a majority of direct sales consultants are women entering (or re-entering) the work force to have a source of income not dependent on their spouse.

2. To **structure** the day as one sees fit – working the hours you can and desire to. Especially for Beth, as a working mom, the flexibility of working in direct sales is very important to her.

3. To **engage** in a community – we are all looking for a sense of belonging … being part of a direct sales organization can provide an extended "family".

33

The specific reason you decided to enter the direct sales world is actually less important than the fact that **you keep your reason in mind at all times**. The next 100 days are not going to be easy. You may be tested, challenged ... lonely and frustrated. That comes with the territory of starting something new and pushing yourself beyond your comfort zone.

One way to stay on course and not lose heart, is to keep in mind WHY you are doing what you are doing.

We even suggest writing down and reading, and rereading every day the reason you went into direct sales in the first place.

Here is one sales consultant's writing which she keeps in her purse and reviews every morning:

I WANT TO HAVE A SOURCE OF MONEY THAT IS DEPENDENT ONLY ON MY EFFORTS. I WANT TO BE ABLE TO HELP THOSE I LOVE IF AND WHEN THEY NEED ME. I WANT TO BE MY OWN BOSS AND SEE THE DIRECT BENEFITS OF MY EFFORTS.

By keeping in the forefront of your mind exactly **WHY** you are taking on the challenge of being an entrepreneur, you are less likely to falter. People have an enormous ability to outperform even optimistic expectations **when their objectives are sufficiently important to them.** By reminding yourself every day **why** you are doing what you are doing, you reinforce your fortitude and improve the chances of meeting (or exceeding) your goals.

36

OUR SUGGESTION

Experts suggest that in thinking about your WHY, you go deeper than just contemplating additional money. What is it that you will do with that money?

Fund a family vacation, as Beth hopes? Start saving for a college education? Help an elderly parent? Satisfy a desire to travel?

Money is great, of course, but what really keeps people focused and on course is the WHY they want that money … and how they intend to use that money to improve their life!

37

GOAL SETTING

Not all successful people are goal setters. Some do not set specific targets but rather keep the big picture in mind and do their best every single day. Others set very specific goals – sometimes even weekly.

We have heard all the points for and against goal setting. Our advice, given that you are a new entrepreneur, is that you **do set goals** – realistic, incremental goals for each month of your first 100 days. Here are some suggestions:

Goals in Month #1: "(A) to become totally conversant with my product, (B) to study my company's training materials and participate in whatever seminars, webinairs and training sessions they provide, (C) to practice my presentation to prospective customers (preferably in front of a mirror) no less than five times, (D) to make a detailed list on a spread sheet of all the people I intend to contact within my first 100 days – this spread sheet (we like Excel) should identify contact information, prospect responses, follow-ups and so on, (E) to hold a launch party or event for friends and family."

Goals in Month #2: "(A) to follow up with everyone who attended my launch party/event, asking for constructive suggestions, bookings and referrals, (B) to explore marketing and advertising in local newspapers and online, to post flyers and try other outreach ideas, (C) to read as much as I can on prospecting and networking, (D) to book as many meetings or parties as possible but not less than the numbers suggested in my company training materials, (E) to achieve the number of sales suggested in my company's manual or starter kit – targeting incentive reward levels."

Goals in Month #3: "(A) to follow up with everyone to whom I made a sale, make sure they got their product and are happy with it, (B) to update my spread sheet with new names and follow-up dates for customers, (C) to ask satisfied customers for referrals, (D) to contact 10 of the referred individuals, (E) to achieve the incentive-level number of sales identified in my manual or starter kit for month #3."

The goals we indicated above are arbitrary, of course. The point is to identify specific targets to be achieved within specific time frames. The process of doing that – and then constantly focusing on your monthly goals – will in and of itself be a great step to moving you forward in your first 100 days.

By the way, a great book with lots of ideas for goal-setting and prioritizing is:

Eat That Frog!, by Brian Tracy
(Berrett-Koehler, 2007)

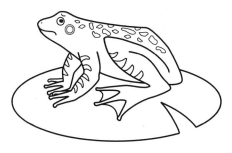

TO DO LISTS

We are a big believer in To Do lists. Some people call them "To Accomplish" lists to highlight the point that each item you check off your list moves you closer to **accomplishing** your goals.

To Do lists are nothing more than a way to stay organized. We suggest you make your list either the evening before each day, or early the morning of – so that you know exactly what you want to accomplish every single day.

"Every effective executive works from a daily list. It is the most powerful tool ever discovered for maximum productivity.

"When you create your daily list, you begin by writing down every single task you intend to complete over the course of the day. The rule is that you will increase your efficiency by 25 percent the very first day that you start using a list. This means that you will get two extra hours of productive time in an eight-hour day ... You can bring order out of chaos faster with a list than with any other time management tool."

Time Power: A Proven System for Getting More Done,
Brian Tracy

BACK TO BILLY AND BETH

"Is there something you aren't telling me about you and the lawn guy?"

Well he did have great shoulders.

"Don't be ridiculous … I am just making a list of every person I know who could possibly be a candidate to buy my products."

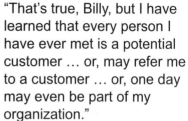

"That's true, Billy, but I have learned that every person I have ever met is a potential customer … or, may refer me to a customer … or, one day may even be part of my organization."

"But you hardly know him."

45

"Your organization??"

"Billy, I am getting ahead of myself here but one day I may have people who work for me … whose sales revenues are shared with me."

46

Perhaps you have already had a discussion with those people who may be impacted by your going into direct sales. Some may be supportive, others may have reservations.

Since the next 100 days may be a bit tough, if you have not already had this discussion, it's time! Experts cite over and over that one element of success in direct sales is the support of a consultant's family and friends.

Be sure to explain why you are doing this, and how much it means to you. And ask for their support and assistance.

SPREAD SHEETS

As you have read, Beth is starting to make a spread sheet of everyone she knows who might be a candidate to buy from her, or refer her to someone who will.

Now is the time to be creative. Make a list of every single person you know. Friends and family are first of course. But then you need to expand outward (think of the concentric circles which appear when you throw a stone in a pond). Casual acquaintances. People you buy from – service people and retailers. People you met at Little League, your church, your school. All of these people are candidates to buy your product.

LET'S TAKE A LOOK AT WHAT BETH'S SPREAD SHEET LOOKS LIKE

PROSPECTS

Name	John Jones	Cara Yelti
Address	57 Glenbrook St, Anytown USA	42 Roundlake Rd, Anytc
Home Phone	203-555-5501	914-555-7388
Cell Phone	203-555-7306	914-555-2219
Email	jjones@email.com	cyelti@email.com
How I know this person	Aimee's Friend	Dad's Neighbor
Date of 1st Contact	8/13	8/15
Summary of Conversation		Interested in hearing more
If Sold, Quantity		8 Sold
Need for Refill	N/A	N/A
Other Follow Up		
Date of Follow Up	9/13	8/31
Referred By	N/A	N/A
Referred Me To	Sara Sibeto	
Date "Thank You" Sent	8/20	

The point of Beth's spread sheet is to help her keep track of every person she speaks with, and of the people she is going to speak with.

It also summarizes conversations - whether a sale was made and if not, why not, what an appropriate follow-up would be ... and so on. This spread sheet is critical to the success of BETH INC.

Perhaps you are tentative about creating a list of everyone you have ever met. Perhaps you are unsure about contacting people like the person who does your lawn. Or, someone you casually met at say a Little League game.

Well now is the time for us to tell you about a very important fact about success in direct selling.

IF YOU BELIEVE IN YOUR PRODUCT, YOU SHOULD FEEL GOOD ABOUT OFFERING IT TO PEOPLE

Perhaps the largest single difference between great salespeople and those who don't make it, is that the former do not feel anxious or guilty about approaching people.

Great salespeople believe in the value of their products and by introducing their products to others, they feel that they are spreading the word about something of interest and value (like when you tell a friend about a great book or movie). In addition, top direct sales consultants operate with the mindset that by offering someone a direct sale, they are saving that person the trouble of trying to find a comparable product in a store, or online (making his or her life easier).

Great salespeople realize that not everyone is a buyer. They are not insulted when people say "NO." They check back with that person at a later date, and they realize that in large part sales is a numbers game.

At first you may get 10 "NO's" for every "YES." As you get better at your message and communication (how you engage with prospective customers), and better at creating targeted lists of who to contact (those most likely to buy), you may get 7 "NO's" for every "YES." But, you will probably always get more "NO's" than "YES's."

Let me repeat: Sales is a numbers game. The more people you speak with, the greater your odds of making a sale.

Sure your communication is important. And understanding how to sell is, of course, critical. But, do not be dissuaded from approaching people because you don't think you are a natural sales person. For the most part, great salespeople are just those who speak with the most people. Experienced salespeople will convert more prospects than a newbie, but in general their aptitude is for accumulating names, building relationships and eliciting referrals.

One expert told us a cute (yet profound) saying:

"There are only three types of NO:

1. ***No**, not now*
2. ***No**, not ever*
3. *I **know** (pun intended) someone who might be interested."*

One point is that in sales, "NO's" are a fact of life. Get used to them.

A lot of sales trainers try to persuade you to look for every way possible to turn a NO into a YES. We caution against that. There is nothing worse that a salesperson who won't take NO for an answer.

Respect the person across the table from you. She may not be in a position to buy. Or, she may just not need your product.

By treating every prospect with respect, you earn their trust and you never know when they might (on their own) change their mind ... or refer you to someone who is a buyer.

Making a sale also has a tempo to it. In your first 100 days you may feel pressure to make sales right away, and perhaps you will be able to sell to your friends and family. But, you will never be able to sustain a business selling to just your friends and family.

Eventually you will want to sell to people who you have only met casually ... or are just meeting for the first time.

THE TEMPO OF MAKING A SALE

The biggest mistake that new salespeople make is bringing to a sales conversation the attitude that they MUST make the sale at the first encounter.

Inexperienced salespeople are anxious to succeed (like most of us) and so they press, hoping to achieve a sale on the first try. Sometimes they do make a sale BUT most often a sale takes more than one contact with the prospective buyer.

Especially when dealing with someone you don't know, the process of making a sale involves what we call conversion stages ... points you need to establish to turn a prospect into a willing customer.

HERE ARE THE CONVERSION STAGES

1. **BUILDING RAPPORT WITH THE PROSPECT**

2. **GETTING THE PROSPECT COMFORTABLE WITH YOUR PRODUCT**

3. **HELPING THE PROSPECT SEE THE REASONS FOR BUYING YOUR PRODUCT**

4. **GETTING THE PROSPECT TO SEE THE BENEFITS OF BUYING YOUR PRODUCT <u>NOW</u>**

You will not make a sale until you have achieved all of the indicated stages. And here is the critical point:

It often takes time to convert a prospect at each one of our four stages.

One way to think about selling is to think of yourself as a buyer.

Imagine that someone asks you for a meeting so that she can tell you about a new product she is selling. You barely know this person but you decide to listen as a courtesy.

1. You are a little suspicious – we all are a tad uncomfortable with people we don't know.

2. No matter what she is selling, you are a little dubious about the product.

3. Even if you are convinced that the person and product are "above board," you are not sure it is for you.

4. And finally, if you do decide to try it, you may delay or defer the decision as to when.

If the above is a fair description of how you would react to a person contacting you, you can understand the importance of our CONVERSION STAGES. To turn, or convert, a prospect into a buyer, you need to address each of the four questions that this person (a hypothetical YOU) will have before committing to buy (if ever).

And achieving those conversions CAN TAKE TIME!!

Each person is different of course but for most people there is a lag between the first time they meet you or hear about your product ... and the time when they decide how they feel about you and your product.

Did you know that great marketers believe that with a new product or brand, most buyers need SEVEN IMPRESSIONS before they will try the product. In other words, they must have seen SEVEN ads, or heard about the product from SEVEN people, or seen something about it SEVEN times before they will try it.

Each impression is an incremental step toward achieving our CONVERSION STAGES.

THE BIG POINT IS THAT MOST PEOPLE ARE GOING TO BECOME CUSTOMERS GRADUALLY. THAT IS WHY YOU CANNOT BE IMPATIENT OR DISCOURAGED IF YOU DO NOT MAKE SALES ON YOUR FIRST TRY (IN MOST SITUATIONS YOU WILL NOT).

ONE OF THE REASONS PEOPLE LOSE HEART DURING THE FIRST 100 DAYS OF THEIR DIRECT SALES JOURNEY IS THAT THEY DO NOT UNDERSTAND THIS POINT.

YOU NOW GET IT ... SO YOU ARE ALREADY AHEAD OF MOST NEWCOMERS TO THE BUSINESS.

CONGRATULATIONS!!!

"Great salespeople understand that the sales process takes time. They know that not everyone is a buyer, but that since you never know who is and who isn't, you must treat every prospect with the same courtesy and determination to make a sale.

"When you get a 'no' you try to convert it into a 'maybe.' When you get a 'maybe,' you try to convert it into a 'you can call me another time.' When you get a 'call me another time,' you try to convert it into a specific date. When you get a specific date, you try to convert it into a positive sales event – where the prospect finally sees the benefit to her of owning your product. And so on.

"Often sales is like doing a jigsaw puzzle. After struggling with piece after piece, you finally arrive at a beautiful picture."

Jim Randel, founder of **The Skinny On** book series

73

"You know, Billy, making sales is like doing a jigsaw puzzle."

"You mean it takes time, you get frustrated, you wonder why you bought the dumb puzzle in the first place, and your dog eats pieces that drop on the floor?"

74

75

LET'S RECAP WHAT WE HAVE LEARNED SO FAR:

1. SALES IS A NUMBERS GAME. MOST PEOPLE WILL SAY "NO" AT LEAST AT FIRST.

2. TO BE SUCCESSFUL AT SALES, YOU NEED TO SPEAK WITH LOTS OF PEOPLE. THAT MEANS YOU CANNOT HESITATE APPROACHING PEOPLE YOU BARELY KNOW, OR DON'T KNOW AT ALL. IF YOU BELIEVE IN YOUR PRODUCT, YOU ARE DOING THEM A SERVICE BY OFFERING IT TO THEM .

3. SALES TAKES TIME. IN ORDER TO CONVERT A PROSPECT INTO A BUYER, YOU NEED TO TRAVERSE EACH OF OUR FOUR CONVERSION STAGES.

76

OK, we have learned a lot so far and as far as newcomers to the business go, you are already ahead of about 90% of them. Well done.

Let's take a little break before we jump back into our learning ... want to hear a joke about salespeople?

I will take your silence as a "YES" (see how this sales thing works!!).

OK, well two salespeople work for a shoe company. The shoe company decides that it wants to open new territories so it sends the salespeople to a Polynesian island where it has never sold any shoes.

The first salesperson returns after one day:

"Are you nuts," she says, "we will never sell shoes there. The people don't wear any shoes."

The second salesperson calls after one day:

"We are going to do great here. No one has any shoes!"

Good one, huh?

Well perhaps not a gut-buster but you know what, there is a point there. Good salespeople find opportunities in a lot of different places. That is why it is so important that you begin your first 100 days by making a list of everyone you have ever met. You never know who will be a prospect for your product or, who will know someone who is.

The theme of the shoe joke is that any person not presently using your product is someone that may buy from you.

Here is some advice for finding prospective customers:

1. Join clubs, associations and organizations to meet people.

2. Hold or sponsor parties, events or meetings to introduce yourself and your new venture to others.

3. Wear pins, buttons or other visible items identifying what you do – people may ask about your pin which is, of course, a great opening for a conversation.

4. Give away items with your name and product on it – pads or pens, for example, that you can give out to people you encounter.

5. Engage people – you never know who you are standing next to in the supermarket line. Be respectful of their privacy but there's nothing wrong with a smile and "hello." You never know what that might lead to!!

"It's important to recognize that everyone is a customer...."

The One Minute Entrepreneur
Blanchard, Hutson and Willis

81

HOW TO MEASURE YOUR SUCCESS IN DAYS 1 - 100?

82

NOT BY SALES!!

You need to set realistic measures of your success in your first 100 days. We are most interested in the foundation you are building for sales in the future.

Here are some ways we suggest you measure your success in your first 100 days:

1. Knowledge about your product.

2. Poise and comfort in making your presentation to a prospective customer.

3. The development of a spread sheet and other tools for facilitating the growth of your business.

4. The number of names on your spread sheet.

5. The creating of strategies for meeting people.

6. The steps you have taken to improve your skills – e.g, obtaining books about sales or registering to attend seminars or workshops.

7. The number of associations you have joined to meet people, and the other networking opportunities you have created for yourself.

8. The holding of a launch party (or parties) or, the setting up of event or, one-to-one meetings to introduce you and your product.

9. The number of times someone has said "you can call me in a month" – that is a door to a sale.

10. The skill sets you acquire to facilitate your evolution as an entrepreneur - putting in place systems to handle the growth of your business.

In your first 100 days you are building the foundation for a great house. A beautiful house with everything just the way you want it. But, before you get to the decorating and all the fun stuff, you have to dig a foundation – get a little dirty and dusty, and occasionally hit a rock as you create the space for your foundation.

There will be setbacks in your first 100 days. There may even be a few "failures" – e.g. when someone says "not interested, not now, not ever!" No problem ... that comes with the territory of being an entrepreneur.

As Winston Churchill said:

"Success is the ability to go from failure to failure with enthusiasm."

We would now like to take you into a VERY important area for success in direct sales:

REFERRALS

As you will recall from our stages of conver
first stage is for a prospect to get comfortable \
as a person. When any of us meets someone
first time, we can't help but be a little cautious
just human nature and part of the survival instinct.

The best way to break down this normal caution is to
be introduced to someone by another person. That
is what referrals are all about.

Great salespeople get very good at getting referrals.
Here is an example of a sales conversation that
Sharon (our consultant friend) is making to her
acquaintance (Sue).

"Sue, thanks for your time."

"My pleasure, Sharon. I'm sorry that I'm not a customer for your products but it was nice spending time with you."

88

**WATCH WHAT
HAPPENS NEXT!**

89

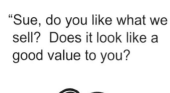

90

91

AN ASIDE: THE FEAR OF BEING PUSHY

Good for Sharon … asking for a referral from Sue.

Many new sales consultants hesitate to ask for what they want. First of course ask for a purchase. If that does not work, ask for a referral.

Some consultants are fearful that they are being pushy. Here is something ironic:

People who worry about being pushy usually aren't. These people are sensitive to others and therefore rarely cross the line from being assertive (good) to being pushy (bad).

One expert suggests that you need to be "gracefully assertive" and if you don't ask for what you want (a sale or referral), "you are deciding for the person you are speaking with ... assuming a NO when you might get a YES."

"Great, thanks. Do you mind giving me her name and having me say I know you?"

"Sure, her name is Jenny Williams. I don't have her number but it is listed. Please don't say that I am recommending anything but yes, you can of course say you know me."

THAT LITTLE EXCHANGE IS A BIG DEAL. SUE WAS NOT A BUYER AND SHARON DID NOT PRESS. AT THE SAME TIME, SHARON HAS THE OPENING TO CALL SUE BACK IN A FEW MONTHS, AND SHARON WILL OF COURSE IMMEDIATELY ENTER THAT INFORMATION IN HER SPREAD SHEET.

THE MORE IMPORTANT EVENT, HOWEVER, WAS SUE GIVING SHARON ANOTHER PERSON'S NAME AND THE "OK" FOR SHARON TO SAY SHE IS "SUE'S FRIEND."

Because Sharon is now able to contact Jenny under the auspices of a relationship with Sue, Sharon has a good start toward making a sale with Jenny.

Sharon has already gone a long way in traversing the first stage of our four conversion stages. Sue's neighbor, Jenny, is much more likely to be open to Sharon since they share a mutual contact (Sue).

Jenny may even assume that Sue has bought products from Sharon. While Sharon should not indicate Sue has (since she has not), the fact is that if Sue was ready to buy, she would in fact buy from Sharon.

If Jenny thinks that Sharon is the kind of honorable person that Sue would buy from, that is a big step toward Jenny trusting Sharon.

REFERRALS ARE A REALLY BIG DEAL IN DIRECT SALES. NO MATTER HOW MANY PEOPLE YOU KNOW, YOU ARE EVENTUALLY GOING TO HAVE TO EXPAND YOUR PROSPECT LIST TO INCLUDE PEOPLE YOU DON'T KNOW.

HOW YOU IDENTIFY THESE PEOPLE AND MAKE THE FIRST CONTACT IS CRITICAL. IF YOU CAN IDENTIFY THEM AND MEET THEM UNDER THE UMBRELLA OF A RELATIONSHIP WITH SOMEONE THEY ALREADY KNOW, YOU HAVE MADE GREAT PROGRESS TOWARD A POSSIBLE SALE.

We have done a lot of homework for you and read most (if not all) of the materials on the subject of referrals.

If you were going to read just one book on the subject of referrals we recommend:

> **Referrals Now!** By Bill Cates
> (McGraw-Hill, 2004).

This is an excellent book which treats referrals as a science – explaining why referrals work and how to get them.

"To create a steady flow of referrals, you must develop a referral mindset. Not a day should go by where you're not working on becoming more referable, planting seeds, asking for referrals, and sending thank you gifts for referrals. Referral marketing must be 'top of mind awareness.'

"You must constantly say to yourself, 'I sell a quality product or service. I deliver incredible service. People like me and trust me. I deserve to get referrals. I serve people so well that they want to refer people to me'."

Referrals Now!

HERE ARE SOME OF THE HIGHLIGHTS FROM CATES' BOOK:

1. The chances of you making a sale to a referral is much higher than to a stranger (even if a very qualified lead).

   In one study of over 5,000 qualified prospects, those obtained by cold calling or other lead generation techniques converted to sales 11% of the time while those obtained by referrals converted to sales over 40% of the time!

2. The cost per lead of a referral is ZERO which obviously compares very well against other mechanisms for establishing qualified leads.

3. There are some people who are great at making a sale but never learn how to convert these customers into sources of referrals – these sales people are leaving LOTS OF MONEY on the table.

4. One of the biggest obstacles to effective selling is tension between the seller and the buyer. When a prospect comes to you through a referral, tension is usually very low, if it exists at all.

5. Never be apologetic in asking for a referral. The more confident you are in asking, the more comfortable the person you are asking will feel … and the more likely she or he will give you the referrals you seek.

Here is how one expert – with a referral mindset – describes her approach to referrals:

"I bring up my request for referrals as a service to my clients. I give them the opportunity to help their friends and colleagues by telling them about me!"

Gloria Gault Geary

The "take away" from this section of our book is that referrals are a great way to build your business. If you are selling a good product and if your service is terrific, then people should be happy to lead you to new prospects.

In your first 100 days, you should read all you can on the subject of referrals and experiment a bit with friends – ask for referrals and see how they react. With time you will become very adept at requesting and getting referrals – which will become a major driver of your success in direct sales!!

OK, IT'S TIME TO TAKE A LITTLE DIVERSION FROM THE SALES PROCESS TO SPEAK ABOUT BUSINESS TECHNIQUES EMPLOYED BY SUCCESSFUL ENTREPRENEURS. IT IS OUR SUGGESTION THAT IF YOU PUT THESE IN PLACE IN YOUR FIRST 100 DAYS YOU ARE ESTABLISHING THE BASE UPON WHICH YOU WILL BUILD YOUR BUSINESS FOR THE LONG TERM.

103

The great thing about entrepreneurs is that they are very motivated to succeed. They know that the results of their efforts will flow directly to them. Because of that, they invest whatever time and energy it takes to get the job done, knowing that they will be the beneficiary of that investment.

Here is a story that makes my point – that illustrates the entrepreneurial approach to business (and to life).

104

Many years ago two tribes in a remote region of the Andes were feuding. One tribe lived in the mountains and the other lived in the lowlands. One day a group of highlanders raided a village of the lowlanders and kidnapped a baby.

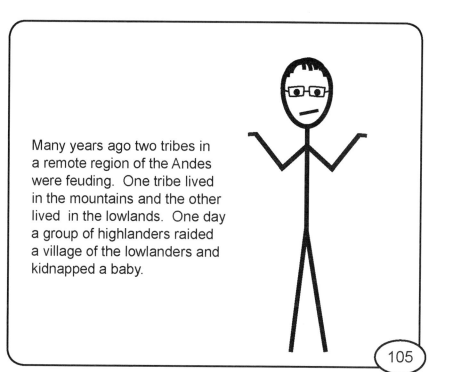

The next day the lowlanders assembled a team of warriors to rescue the baby. But the lowlanders did not know the trails up the mountain, nor were they skilled at mountain climbing. They struggled to ascend the mountain but they only made it half way up. Discouraged, they turned to descend.

Suddenly, to their amazement, they saw a frail woman coming down the mountain with a baby in her arms.

One of the warriors approached her. He recognized her as a woman from his tribe. He realized that the infant was her child.

"How were you able to scale the mountain?! How were you able to find and rescue your child? We are trained warriors. We did our best and could not get even half way up the mountain!"

She answered: "It wasn't your baby."

This story speaks to the entrepreneurial approach.

Although you are just beginning your journey, as an entrepreneur you are building something that can change your life. If you stay the course over the next 100 days ... and beyond... you may end up with a business that provides you with income, freedom, satisfaction, and pride.

Since your business is "your baby," you should be motivated to find ways to work through setbacks ... and there will be plenty of those. But, where others are deterred (the lowlander warriors), you will not be.

WE ARE ABOUT TO GIVE YOU OUR VIEWS ON THE KEYS TO BECOMING A SUCCESSFUL ENTREPRENEUR.

HOWEVER WE WANT TO GIVE YOU THE WHOLE PICTURE. BEING AN ENTREPRENEUR ISN'T EASY. THERE WILL BE TIMES WHEN YOU WILL DOUBT YOUR JOURNEY. WHEN YOU WILL QUESTION WHY YOU CONSIDERED AN ENTREPRENEURIAL VENTURE IN THE FIRST PLACE. WHEN YOU HAVE TO SQUINT TO SEE THE LIGHT AT THE END OF THE TUNNEL.

BUT, YOUR BUSINESS IS "YOUR BABY" AND WHERE THERE'S A WILL, THERE'S A WAY. IF YOU STAY COMMITTED, IF YOU CONTINUE TO DO THE RIGHT THINGS, IF YOU GET UP EVERY TIME YOU GET KNOCKED DOWN, WELL THEN YOU HAVE A SHOT AT SEEING "YOUR BABY" GROW INTO A TALL, STRONG AND THRIVING ADULT!!!

Here are business strategies that entrepreneurs need to adopt:

1. Since you may be starting off with little support, you need to be organized. You most likely don't have an assistant, so you will want to be as effective as possible – that means getting organized.

2. Learn time management skills. Here are our two favorite books on the subject:

   Getting Things Done: The Art of Stress-Free Productivity, David Allen (Penguin, 2002)

   How to Get Control of Your Time and Life, Alan Lakein (Signet, 1973)

3. Create **TO DO LISTS** … know exactly what you choose to accomplish every day. Prioritize what is most important, and highlight those items.

4. Develop routines in your day – the life of an entrepreneur can be lonely. You are on your own and at times you will feel invisible. Give yourself certain touchstones that bring you pleasure and predictability during the day. For example, a daily walk, or 30 minutes to read the news, or coffee with a friend.

5. Promote yourself – this is a hard one for some people. Find ways to tell people about your successes. People gravitate to success stories.

And don't forget to read your WHY statement every day, that reminder as to WHY you are doing what you are doing. That will help keep you focused when you are feeling a little low or lonely. Nothing good comes easy. Stay the course and put one foot in front of the other. Before you know it, you will be surprised at the amount of progress you have made!

Use your first 100 days to build your skills as an entrepreneur: organization, time management, routines, to do lists, and mechanisms for promotion. The time you invest in these efforts will pay returns to you for years to come.

WONDER HOW BETH IS DOING?? ... LET'S CHECK IN.

113

BETH - DAY 33

114

Beth is hitting the wall that almost all new entrepreneurs hit. She has had a succession of rough days and she is struggling a bit. I think I'll give her a call.

"Hi Beth, you don't know me but I have been referred to you by your cousin, Carol. She indicated that she would tell you that I would be calling."

"Yes, she did, Jim. She tells me that you are an expert in starting up a business and know a lot about direct sales. I'm happy you called."

115

116

See how well this REFERRAL thing works!

I know a woman named Becky who knows a woman named Carol who happened to be Beth's cousin. I asked Becky for an introduction to Carol who then introduced me to Beth.

Some people believe that everyone is separated by six contacts (degrees). That everyone knows someone who knows someone who knows someone you are trying to get to. I believe in that.

117

"Beth, being an entrepreneur is tough… especially in the first 100 days. Perhaps you have heard about a force called inertia. It's a law of physics which states that an immovable object tends to stay at rest unless and until acted upon by an outside force.

"What an entrepreneur is trying to do is overcome inertia."

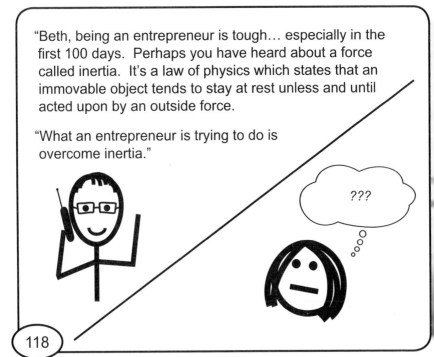

???

118

"Beth, I will take from your silence that you don't have a clue what I am talking about. It must be me ... I often get the same reaction from my wife! Let me try again. ... You are starting a business ... a new direction in life. You are changing the way people perceive you. How they relate to you. You're changing how you spend your days. You're into new waters. That is all frightening and difficult. But here is the point: IT IS SUPPOSED TO BE... IT IS THAT WAY FOR EVERYONE. IF IT WERE EASY, EVERYONE COULD DO IT!!"

"I appreciate what you are saying but maybe I don't have the right stuff to make it in this business… perhaps I jumped into this a little quickly."

121

122

"Hi, Beth... I'm Jim, may I come in?"

123

"Beth, I know that you're wondering about your decision to get into direct sales. That's normal – especially in the first month or two. But, it's too early for you to make any judgments yet. I do suggest that new entrepreneurs gauge their progress, but only after about six months. One month is much too soon."

"I appreciate that, Jim, but I have very little to show for my first month in the business."

124

"You may have little to show by way of sales. But, what about your familiarity with your product, and the systems you have put into place to grow your prospect list? And, what you've learned about referrals, networking and sales?"

"Yes, I guess I am making progress … but none of that puts money in my pocket."

125

"Beth, if you judge your success in your first few months by how much money you make, then you're going to be disappointed. You're planting something here … creating something that will bring you returns for many years to come. You've just put the seeds in the ground ... it's too soon to be expecting beautiful flowers."

"Jim, I know a little bit about you. You've been a successful entrepreneur. Maybe you can't relate to what I'm talking about."

126

"Well, Beth, I have had some successes but like all entrepreneurs I have had hard times, doubts, fears and anxieties.

"I've had sleepless nights, Beth. I have second-guessed my decisions tons of times. It all comes with the territory of trying to build a business for yourself.

"Beth, you are 33 days into what could be a life-changing experience. Hey, I am not going to sugar coat this … I'm not going to guarantee your success. You have a lot of hard work in front of you.

"But 33 days is not enough time to judge yourself. You have to go at least six months before you can make a realistic evaluation of what you are doing. If at that time you determine that your new venture is not for you, well then, make a change at that time.

"Beth, if you don't give yourself an opportunity to succeed, you will never know what you might have accomplished."

"I appreciate the pep talk, Jim... sorry I suggested that you had not experienced what I was feeling."

"No problem, Beth... just remember that what you are feeling, almost every new entrepreneur in direct sales has also felt. Don't think it's just you!"

"Resilience is one of the most valuable characteristics you can develop in life... That's because no matter how hard you're working, or no matter how great your faith is, at some point you're going to hit a wall. Whether you lead a successful life or not depends on how you deal with that wall.

"The successful person is going to go through the wall, over it, around it, under it – whatever it takes to continue on his journey."

Do You, Russell Simmons
(Gotham, 2008)

I have studied entrepreneurs for 20 years ... and have identified patterns. Very few experience instant success. They keep plugging and are not easily discouraged.

Good entrepreneurs work hard at their salesmanship (is "saleswomanship" a word?).

They realize that the key to any business success is sales.

I have learned a lot from some great salespeople. I would like to share with you some of what I have learned.

THE MOST IMPORTANT WAY TO MAKE A SALE IS TO LEARN TO THINK LIKE A BUYER. NO MATTER HOW POLISHED YOUR SALES PITCH, OR HOW ARTICULATE AND CHARMING YOU ARE, OR HOW TERRIFIC YOUR PRODUCT IS, IF THE IDEA OF OWNING YOUR PRODUCT DOES NOT HIT YOUR PROSPECTIVE BUYER'S HOT SPOT, THEN ALL THE OTHER STUFF IS MEANINGLESS.

TO BE A GREAT SALESPERSON YOU NEED TO THINK LIKE A BUYER.

To understand your buyer you need to listen. That is why many experts hate the expression "sales pitch" or "presentation." They feel that the appropriate word is "conversation" to connote a two-sided exchange.

Too many new salespeople get so wrapped up in what they are saying, they don't pay close enough attention to what their prospective customer is saying! That is a huge mistake because if you listen carefully to your prospect, she will usually give you a road map into what is in her mind!

You want to be a great salesperson? Learn to be a great listener!

"Power lives more in listening than in talking. In fact, listening may be the key skill of a successful person."

The Corporate Mystic, Hendricks and
Ludeman (Signet, 1999)

If you want to learn more about the importance of listening, go to the library and read Chapter 12 of one of the most famous self-improvement books ever written, **How to Win Friends and Influence People** written in 1936 by Dale Carnegie. This chapter, titled "Be a Good Listener" makes the point that often the easiest and most effective way to win someone over is TO LISTEN TO WHAT THEY ARE SAYING!!! Duh…

In Carnegie's book he speaks about the power of great listeners.

Sigmund Freud, the world-famous psychologist was a great listener. Here is how someone described speaking with Freud:

"Never had I seen such concentrated attention. There was none of that piercing 'soul penetrating gaze' business. His eyes were mild and genial. His voice was low and kind. His gestures were few. But the attention he gave me, his appreciation of what I said … was extraordinary. You've got no idea what it meant to be listened to like that."

When you listen so that you can see the world from a buyer's eyes, you begin to understand a critical point about selling:

PEOPLE BUY TO SATISFY AN EMOTIONAL DESIRE OR NEED.

138

"People don't buy logically. They buy emotionally, and then justify their purchases logically."

Tom Hopkins, well-known expert on selling

139

In speaking with direct selling expert, Nicki Keohohou (the CEO and founder of the Direct Selling Women's Alliance), we learned about the difference between "internal" listening and "heart-centered™" listening.

Nicki draws a distinction between people who listen to others only with their mind … and those who listen with their heart. The former are always thinking about how to fix the speaker's problem ("thereby presuming that the speaker even has a problem," says Nicki) while the latter are engaging with the speaker – trying to understand the speaker's feelings and needs.

Nicki believes that by training yourself to be a "heart-centered™" listener you will become a much better seller because you will **engage** with your prospect on a deeper level than will the person who listens only with her ears.

INTERNAL LISTENING	HEART-CENTERED LISTENING™
Focus on ourselves, waiting for our turn to talk	Focus on speaker, all else is blocked out
Listening to our own inner voice	Listen to speaker's words and their meaning
Making judgments, opinions	Understanding speaker's feelings and needs
Waiting impatiently for speaker to finish	Body expresses interest through eye contact, focus, etc.
Interpreting from own experience, perspectives	Unattached to own experience, perspectives
Looking for solutions, advice, how to fix it	Trusting that the person can solve by finding own answers
Creates no real communication or connection	Creates trust, connection, and validation

(Thanks to Nicki for sharing this chart with us.)

OK, so what are some of the emotions that cause people to buy?

Joy
Love
Awe
Anticipation
Fear
Surprise
Excitement

The goal as a salesperson is to find your customer's touch point – where she will react emotionally to your product or service.

Great salespeople will tailor a sales conversation to address an emotional desire or need. Will your product make a customer feel younger and thus joyful? Will your product cause a customer to be more attractive to the opposite sex and ignite feelings of love and anticipation? Will your product cause others to be in awe of your customer?

Negative emotions can be touched as well. Will your product reduce your customer's fear or disappointment?

By listening very carefully to your prospective buyer, by watching for body language, by thinking like your buyer, you start to get a sense of what will motivate your prospect to buy. Eventually, you will determine which emotions you need to engage to ignite your prospective customer's interest.

Great salespeople know that by gaining an understanding of the person across the table from you, you enhance your chances of a successful conversation.

"Seek first to understand."

The Seven Habits of Highly Effective People, Stephen R. Covey (Free Press, 2004)

"My selling purpose is to help people get the good <u>feelings</u> they want -- about what they bought, and about themselves."

The One Minute Sales Person, Johnson & Wilson (William Morrow, 1984)

145

Does it feel manipulative to try to touch a person's emotions in selling them a product?

Do you ever feel like you are pushing something on people who really don't need it, or can't afford it?

146

THE ETHICS OF SALES

Some people think that sales people are unethical, fast-talking pushers. But, in our view that is rarely the truth.

Sales is about convincing someone that she would be better off with your product than with the money in her pocket. Great salespeople do not push a product on people who will not really benefit from it … or, can't afford it. Great salespeople are in business for the long-term, and they know that eventually their success will depend upon a universe of satisfied and happy customers.

In your first 100 days you may feel pressure to sell. You may feel pressure to justify your decision to go into direct sales to your family and friends. AND, you will want self-validation for your decision.

But, notwithstanding the pressures you feel, you can never waiver from your sense of integrity and propriety. Treat every prospective customer as you would treat a family member or friend. Heck, just follow The Golden Rule. There is nothing wrong with introducing a great product to people and suggesting the ways in which it can help them. Just do so in a way that is caring, forthright and patient … and you will do just fine!

During your first 100 days you will want to hold tight onto not only your sense of integrity **but also your sense of humor**!

As we have been stating throughout this book, you are likely to be tested in your first few months. There will almost assuredly be frustrations and setbacks.

You will need to learn to persist and persevere against setbacks.

Persistence is huge! No one ever fails until they stop trying!

"90% of the reason for my success is that I just kept showing up."

Woody Allen

WHY PERSISTENCE WORKS

Persistence is not just some "feel good" theory. There are reasons persistence works:

1. The longer you work at something, the better you get at it. Over time, your sales conversations will improve. Your ability to determine what it is that your prospect is actually looking for, and how to tailor your comments, gets better and better.

2. The longer you work at something, the more people are impressed. The first time you meet a prospective customer, she may be interested in your product but not yet a buyer. But, how about when you come back six months later: "Hi, Mary, I have sold a lot of products since I saw you last and have many happy customers ...I thought you'd like to hear about how the products are helping others."

3. The longer you work at something, the more opportunities you will have to take your business to the next level. If you operate (as I do) with the assumption that we all get a certain number of great opportunities in life, you realize that unless you are "in the game" all the time, those opportunities may sail by while you are sleeping. In other words, the longer you work at something, the greater the probability that you will have some amazing opportunities fall into your lap.

4. The longer you work at something, the more the numbers start to work in your favor. As we have discussed, sales is a numbers game. Over time, your prospects will increase exponentially as you make more customers happy. At first, and most likely in your initial 100 days, it will be hard to discern the progress you are making in the numbers game. But if you create happy customers, they will talk. And one person will tell another who will tell another and so on and so on.

By understanding and accepting that your first 100 days will be challenging, you are buffering yourself for whatever happens. You have primed your mind for the potential frustrations and setbacks of any new venture. You are on alert and ready for the headwinds. You are better able to persist and activate your creativity as necessary.

151

There is a Latin saying:

PRAEMONITUS PRAEMUNITUS.

Any guesses what that means?

It means **FOREWARNED is FOREARMED**.

You have been warned – the first 100 days may be challenging. And so you are armed and ready.

152

Just the fact that you have read this book has increased the likelihood that you will be successful in your direct sales venture – not just in the first 100 days of course, but in the years ahead.

SO, CONGRATULATIONS ... YOU HAVE ALREADY MOVED YOURSELF FORWARD!

LET'S CHECK IN ON BETH

"I'm not quite finished yet … I'm at Panel 157 but I must say it touched on many of the experiences I had in my first 100 days in the business. I wish I had this book while I was going through that period … it would have made my journey that much easier."

157

"Well I wish your journey had been a bit easier for your sake … but I sure am happy you stuck with it .. however you did it."

158

I'm happy to report that Beth stuck out her first 100 days and beyond. She is now in the middle of her second year in the business and as you could see, she was able to pay for a family vacation for she, Billy and their kids.

I sure am happy for Beth!

As a matter of fact, Beth called me recently and suggested I put together a summary of this book to recap the top ten points a person in direct sales should know in her/his first 100 days... so, my summary follows.

But, just before I leave you, let me say that I hope you find the desire and will to get through the next 100 days. I am not going to tell you that direct sales is for everyone and you may eventually conclude that it is not for you. But, I do believe that only after using your best efforts for some minimum period, can you make a good decision about your future ... and that period is more than 100 days!

GOOD LUCK AND BEST WISHES FROM ALL OF US AT *SKINNY ON BOOKS*!!

TOP TEN TIPS FOR THE FIRST 100 DAYS IN DIRECT SALES

#1: Write down WHY you want to be in direct sales. Read your WHY statement every day – maybe a few times a day. By staying focused on YOUR GOALS you strengthen your resolve to deal with the challenge of your first 100 days.

#2: Remember that it is not easy to be an entrepreneur. You are building an enterprise that can give you the flexibility and freedom to live your life as you want.

Be business-like in the approach to your new career. Be sure you understand all of your company's written materials. Read books on the basics of running your own business.

The great news is that you have no boss but you. If you are not happy with your income, look in the mirror and complain to the person you see there.

#3: By preparing yourself for the challenge ahead, you buffer yourself against setbacks. By knowing that there will be disappointments in the first 100 days, your mind is ready.

When disappointments come, instead of your mind going "OH NO, OH NO," your mind goes "AHA, I have been expecting you … I did not know how you would show up, but I knew you would be here eventually. I will figure out a way to get past you!"

#4: Be realistic as to your objectives for the first 100 days. The measures you set for yourself should not be tied to sales, but rather to the relationships you establish and the foundation you build for future success.

Here are some objectives you should aspire to in your first 100 days: learning about your products, polishing your sales conversation, creating a spread sheet for contact and follow-up, making lists of prospects, holding launch parties and events, spreading the word to friends and family about what you are doing and asking for their assistance, develop "give-away" items that can break the ice with strangers. And so on and so on.

#5: Ask for referrals. Even if you do not make one sale in your first 100 days, you can build your future by developing the ability to ask for referrals. Remember all the reasons that referrals work: low-tension selling, low (zero) cost of acquisition of a lead, and higher conversion rates.

#6: Tell yourself every day that you must be patient. Far too many people throw in the towel in the first few months of direct sales because their time line is all wrong. Other than people who love and want to support your new enterprise, most people need to be persuaded gradually to try a new product or service. If you rush the tempo, if you forget the four conversion stages, you may be overbearing and appear anxious, thereby losing a good customer.

#7: Invest as much of your first 100 days as possible educating yourself. Great salespeople aren't born that way. They develop their sales skills over time. They learn to listen (think Freud) and touch people's emotions with their comments. Read everything you can. Attend seminars. Speak with successful salespeople and ask for guidance. You don't need to reinvent the wheel. Learn from those who have already been successful in direct sales.

#8: Join every association, organization and club you can. The larger your network (the people who know you), the more likely you will be successful.

Reminder (for the 10th time): sales is a numbers game. The more people you touch, the more people buyers you will have.

#9: Overperform! The world is full of people who over promise and underperform. Be the opposite ... be understated in your promise, and overstated in your performance. In whatever opportunities you have in your first 100 days to show off your customer service and follow-through, do so. Give people a reason to start talking about you! You will be surprised how quickly one person tells another who tells another and so on. The power of over performance cannot be overstated!

#10: Commit to treating people honorably and with sensitivity to their situation. There may be some people who would like to buy from you but are not in a financial position to do so. Do not push those people. Do not persuade people to buy your product who will not benefit from using or owning it. Although you may feel pressure to make sales in your first 100 days, do not vary the ethical standards you set for yourself. In the final analysis, you can always make money. But, you can never get back the harm you may do by acting less than 100% honorably.

CONCLUSION

That concludes our **Skinny Book**. We hope that you have enjoyed it. As with all of our books, we would love to hear your comments.

Please let me know what you think.

jrandel@theskinnyon.com

With warmest wishes,

Jim Randel

BIBLIOGRAPHY

A to Z of Direct Selling, Andrew Nelson (Author House, 2004)

Believe, Nicki Keohohou (CD)

Build it Big: 101 Insider Secrets from Direct Selling Experts, DSWA (Dearborn, 2005)

Direct Selling in the United States (Direct Selling Education Assn., 1995)

Don't Worry, Make Money, Richard Carlson (Hyperion, 1997)

Getting Things Done, David Allen (Penguin, 2001)

Home-Based Business ... Is it for Me? (ndsu.edu)

Making Millions in Direct Sales, Michael Malaghan (McGraw-Hill, 2005)

The First 90 Days: Critical Success Strategies, Michael Watkins (Harvard Press, 2003)

The Seven Habits of Highly Effective People, Stephen R. Covey (Free Press, 2004)

Time Power, Brian Tracy (Amacon, 2007)

Referrals Now!, Bill Cates (McGraw-Hill, 2004)

The Greatest Networker in the World, John Milton Fogg (Three River Press, 1997)

The One Minute Entrepreneur, Blanchard and Huston (Broadway, 2008)

The One Minute Sales Person, Johnson and Wilson (William Morrow, 1984)

Ultimate Guide to Direct Selling, Phelps (Advantage Media, 2008)

Pssst ... get
the skinny on™
life's most
important lessons

Remember to

visit theskinnyon.com and join
The Skinny On™ community to:

- Keep your book current
  with free web updates

- Sign up for **The Skinny On™**
  e-letter

- View upcoming topics and
  suggest areas of research
  for new titles

- Read excerpts from any of
  The Skinny On™ books

- Purchase other **The Skinny On™**
  titles

- Learn how to write for
  The Skinny On™!

Connect with us on:

www.theskinnyon.com

702 -
481 -
583)